Our Garden of Kindness

Copyright © 2023 Junior League of Tulsa

Printed in the United States of America

ISBN: 9798218060305 (hardback)

Published by: Joseph's Ministry, LLC

www.josephsministryllc.com

Written by: Annette LaFortune Murray

Illustrator: Ariana Jakub Brandes

Presented by the Junior League of Tulsa

www.jltulsa.org

All rights reserved. This book or any portion thereof may not be reproduced or used in any manner whatsoever without the express written permission of the Junior League of Tulsa except for the use of brief quotations in a book review.

Our Garden of Kindness

Written by: Annette LaFortune Murray

Illustrated by: Ariana Jakub Brandes

Presented by the Junior League of Tulsa in honor of

100 years of women building a better Tulsa

This book is dedicated to all volunteers working to make our communities better and to all future volunteers. May you change the world one person at a time.

Foreword

Volunteerism is vital to making a difference in one's community. As the Junior League of Tulsa located in Tulsa, Oklahoma celebrates its centennial, our organization wanted to convey that message to the next generation through a children's book. Annette LaFortune Murray has crafted a darling story conveying how volunteering can be not only meaningful, but also rewarding and fun. Ariana Jakub Brandes accompanies this delightful book with playful imagery, making this story truly a joy to experience. We hope reading this book inspires you and your loved ones!

Christina Oden
President 2022-23
Junior League of Tulsa

"Look at all the work going on in the field," Mommy said as she stopped her bicycle, waiting for Max, Cassie, and Mai to catch up.

Everyone stood to watch the workers and trucks clear the field. "When will we see the garden?" Mai asked.

"It won't be too long. When the community garden is ready, Super Sprouts Camp will help plant vegetables. Would you like to help?" asked Mommy.

"Mr. Ahmed is looking for volunteers to help in the garden at camp."

"Yessssssss!!!" screamed the kids.

"Let's race home!" Cassie called.

"Last one home is a stegosaurus!"

In the abandoned lot across the river, adult volunteers loaded trash into dump trucks and trailers.

First, big trucks hauled off the clutter.
Next, bigger trucks full of dirt arrived.

Then, volunteers spread the soil. The messy field was turning into something beautiful: a community garden.

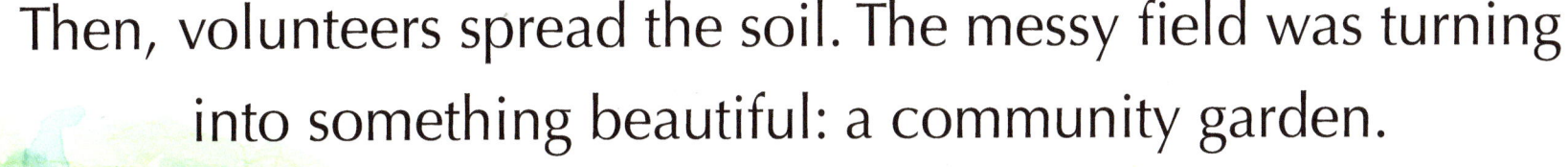

Once summer arrived, Super Sprouts Camp at The Garden of Kindness began.

Mr. Ahmed led the Super Sprouts Camp on Saturdays. Cassie and her new friend, Zara, learned about plants that grow on vines like cucumbers, watermelons, and pumpkins.

Max and Mai's group built containers for herbs.

The green, leafy sage and mint plants smelled like sweet perfume.

Soon, green beans and tomatoes reached up to the sky. Corn and okra stalks crowded each other.

After weeks of volunteering, Mr. Ahmed announced to the Super Sprouts, "Come back next week with your friends and family. We want to show the neighbors how hard you've worked all summer in our community garden. I am so proud of you."

Cassie and Zara fist-bumped and chanted, "Teamwork in the garden is dream work!"

When the community garden was ready to be harvested, the older students in town wanted to surprise the Super Sprouts with a Food Fest.

Two days later, the swim team won the regional meet. The athletes and parents cheered and chanted. The swim meet and the Food Fest were on the same day. What about the surprise for the Super Sprouts?

"Oh no! Winning is great for the swim team, but it's a huge problem for us," Mommy said to Mr. Ahmed.

"Our older students won't be here to put on the surprise party. Should we ask the parents to take over Food Fest?"

Mr. Ahmed agreed, "Parents can cook and arrange a talent show. Let's invite the neighbors who live near our Garden of Kindness. This is their garden, too. After the Super Sprouts arrive and enjoy the surprise, I will ask them to be tour guides for our neighbors."

Mr. Jung made fruit kabobs.

Mr. Tilley made veggie pizza.

Grandma Laura served sno-cones.

As harvest season arrived, parents were busy preparing for Food Fest and the community garden was open to the public.

At the far end of the garden, parents and adults planned a surprise with food, music, games, and prizes.

Mr. Edwards turned his long, flat trailer into a talent show stage.

The Super Sprouts gave tours of the garden for the neighbors. Parents watched children laughing together, talking to new neighbors, and being part of something important.

In the next few years, Cassie, Max, Mai, and Zara began training new Super Sprouts.

"Trying new things helps you make new friends. Volunteering at the community garden makes you feel like you are making a difference in the world," Mai explained. After a few weeks of volunteering, the new Super Sprouts felt like they were making a difference in the world, too.

Glossary

Cheer: To show excitement and clap hands

Community garden: A big garden for sharing

Dream work: When your team works together for a great outcome

Food Fest: A party in the garden with food, music, games, friends, families

Haul: To carry or move something

Herbs: Plant leaves, seeds, or flowers used for flavor in cooking

Kindness: Being helpful or friendly

Neighbor: Someone who lives or works near each other

Soil: Dirt in the ground or earth

Teamwork: When each person in a group does their part to make a difference in the outcome

Vegetable: Plant with a stem, flower, or leaves that you can eat

Vines: Fast-growing plant that creeps on the ground

Volunteer: Someone who helps out on projects or work and does not get paid money

Recommended Reading

Harlem Grown, How One Big Idea Transformed a Neighborhood
by Tony Hillery
Ilustrated by Jessie Hart
(Simon & Schuster/Paul Wiseman Books, 2020)

In Our Garden
by Pat Zietlow Miller
Illustrated by Melissa Crowton
(G.P. Putnam & Sons Books for Young Readers, 2022)

What Grew in Larry's Garden
by Laura Alary
Illustrated by Kass Reich
(Kids Can press, 2020)

100 YEARS OF WOMEN BUILDING A BETTER TULSA

The Junior League of Tulsa, Inc. (JLT) is an organization of women whose mission is to advance women's leadership for meaningful community impact through volunteer action, collaboration, and training. JLT was organized in 1923 and remains committed to working to end the cycle of poverty through hands-on education and community based programs. Below are just a few of our many projects and collaborations over the last century. Our organization has a history of recognizing needs in the community, collaborating, and taking action to influence positive change to improve our community.

1926
Tulsa Children's Medical Center: The original focus of the Junior League Convalescent Center was the caring of children, crippled by and recovering from polio, who sought a facility to aid in rehabilitation. This was the first children's hospital established in Tulsa.

1950s
Tulsa City-County Library Puppet Program: In the 1950s, the JLT partnered with the Tulsa City County Library to create a puppet theater program, which brought stories alive for the children of Tulsa.

1924
Junior League Tea Room: In order to help fund community efforts, JLT established the Tea Room in 1924, which was the first permanent money-raising initiative. Orange Pour Cake was one of the favorite desserts served.

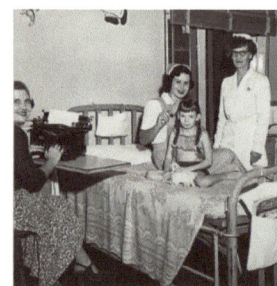

1948
Museum Docent Program: In 1948, JLT established the docent program with Philbrook Museum of Art. The docent program provided opportunities for children in underserved communities to visit the museum and learn about art and art history. In 1957, the docent program expanded to Gilcrease Museum.

1970s
Oxley Nature Center: In the mid-1970s, JLT volunteers helped set up the volunteer nature guide program, started a newsletter, provided publicity, and started the acquisition of materials for the library at the Oxley Nature Center.

1973

Jubilee/Mayfest: In 1973, to commemorate the City of Tulsa's 75th Anniversary, the Junior League of Tulsa's 50th Anniversary, and the Tulsa Philharmonic Society's 25th Anniversary, JLT established what was known as Jubilee '73. The purpose was to produce an arts festival which would bring the performing and visual arts to the people of northeastern Oklahoma, known today as Mayfest.

1994

Tulsa History A to Z: In 1994, the Tulsa Historical Society approached JLT to develop a third-grade Tulsa history curriculum. Thousands of volunteer hours and three years of researching, writing, rewriting, and editing resulted in "Tulsa History A to Z," a resource that is still in use today.

2015 - PRESENT

Street School: In 2015, JLT began a partnership with Street School, the only tuition-free, non-profit, alternative high school in Tulsa to focus on dropout prevention, intervention, and recovery for students in grades 9-12. JLT teaches cooking classes for students participating in Street School's "Culinary Club" with a focus on affordable and nutritious meal options.

1989

Ronald McDonald House: In 1989, JLT helped establish the Ronald McDonald House in Tulsa by raising awareness and funds and implementing a volunteer organization. Recently, JLT members began serving again at Ronald McDonald House Tulsa as part of the Lunches with Love program to provide meals for families battling illness.

2009

Kids in the Kitchen: The Harvest Market, which opened in 2009, served approximately 1,000 low-income families in the Eugene Field neighborhood, which is considered a food desert. The Harvest Market had a grocery store, art studio, classroom, and teaching kitchen where JLT members hosted Kids in the Kitchen workshops and cooking classes for youth and their caregivers.

ABOUT THE AUTHOR

Annette LaFortune Murray is a former member of Junior League of Tulsa (JLT) and an author of children's books. She wrote *ABC, WHAT DO YOU SEE? ROLLING ALONG ROUTE 66*, a non-fiction picture book for ages 5-8, that celebrates the magic along all eight states of America's historic highway. She was an educator and school librarian for 30 years. Annette loves gardening, writing, traveling, and playing pickleball. Four generations of women in Annette's family served their community in Junior League: Gertrude LaFortune (grandmother), Jeanne LaFortune (mother), Suzie Bynum (sister), and Kay Phoenix (sister), and Lea LaFortune (niece/Dallas Junior League).

ABOUT THE ILLUSTRATOR

Ariana Jakub Brandes is an artist and teacher based in Tulsa, OK. Her paintings often incorporate rhythms and patterns observed in nature. She enjoys working with watercolors, wine, pastels, and gouache. Ariana grew up in Trenton, New Jersey where both her grandmother and grandfather kept vegetable gardens in their backyards. She teaches Art at Cascia Hall and has exhibited her work at Tulsa International Airport and various galleries throughout the United States. Her work can be viewed at *www.arianajakub.com* and on Instagram @arianajakub.

CPSIA information can be obtained
at www.ICGtesting.com
Printed in the USA
BVHW091732160223
658687BV00008B/95